bouquet
of
thorny rose

poetry by Sossity Chiricuzio

ECHOBIRD
PRESS

Address inquiries in permission to:
Echobird Press, echobirdpress.com
ISBN 978-1-961370-04-3 | ISBN 978-1-961370-05-0 EPUB

Dedication

For Dorothy, Minnie Bruce, and Alice B.

Table of Contents

Content warning: This collection lives in the body, as does pleasure, trauma, memory, and emotion. These pieces are part of my process to explore, examine, unearth, and name. To revel and celebrate. To mourn and rage. You will find violation and reclamation and naked truths. I've marked the pieces with overt sexual or medical trauma with an *. Please take care of your precious selves.

Oblique fault

The jack in the box sign, his giant crooked head, leering over the fence. Scratchy Bermuda grass and the squeak of sweaty flip flops on 6-year-old feet under a relentless desert sun. A sprinkler, a shower head, a feeling of panic. After an earthquake there is sliding and friction, but fearful. Halted. Trauma instead of a mountain. Silence like holding your breath. The taste of dust.

Dip slip reverse and thrust. Horizontal and vertical. A vast disturbance.

The taste of shame. Sucked dry and spit out.

Upturned face and downturned eyes. Bathroom walls like a cage, crushing inward. Never enough locks for the door. Forced open. Eyes in the keyhole. Slippery porcelain promises that turn into teeth. A tiny mouth. A jaw unhinged, then clenched every night after. A dead sea. A red sea. A mystery. A loss of feeling. A loss of days. Of months and years and memories.

Pressure building, the space between mantle and crust pressed thin and keen.

The core molten through, yanked into tides and droughts.

Molars pressing, pressing, for decades. Muscles strong enough to shear through flesh. Cracking bone instead, exposing my own marrow. Another vulnerable surface. Another loss. Two empty spaces in my lower jaw. Ripped loose and thrown away. Slow healing around a hole deep enough to lose things in. Numb receptacle. Salt water and crossed fingers.

Tonguing the edges of nothing. Tactile sonar. The edge of sensation. The edges of myself.

Come here. Lie down. Take it. Don't cry. Don't tell.

Secret rage narrowing my eyes on the street. Sarcasm like a drawn blade, forged in magma, sheared off sharp and trembling. Fists clenched. Fists slamming into walls. Outward anger driving inward. Knuckles and teeth and words, pressure like a mountain, falling. Mined out, dug and sifted and plundered and left to echo in the dark.

Glass without heat is just sand

there's not many places more awkward to get rowdy
(and by rowdy I mean)
than the backseat of an old station wagon
(naked)
no matter who is lanky
and who is curved

elbows bang
clothes tangle on ankles
sleeves
pulling painful
across a neck
and even with teenage hormones
wailing
you wonder if it's worth it

especially when
this lanky boy
isn't who you're thinking about at all
and the desert night is sprinkled with stars
and the desert wind finds its way through the window
and even as you cough
(all your spit gone to novice kissing)
you know
it could be romantic
if only

but the car is creaking beneath you
because that lanky boy hasn't noticed
you drifting away
any more than he noticed
the actual color of your eyes
and the floor board is flaking away

shades of orange betraying
the fault lines
right there
behind the passenger seat
a hole shaped like a key
melted into a lock

and the desert floor is close enough
to touch
if your arm wasn't caught
in his polo
and
wait
no

he's not done yet
and you wish
it was more than friction
that you could feel something
fiercer than a rough motion

a gradual rise of
almost pleasure
that plateaus
but not a spectacular one
like the mountain framed
in the windshield

just a flat line
in the darkness
waiting for rain

Monsoon

The stars seem closer than usual, even accounting for the fact that I'm up a tree. The storm pushes them towards me, or me to them. The leaves flatten against the wind, dream of flying free. Or maybe that's me again.

Lightning stretches blue white trails across the length of time worn mountains and the back of my eyelids. My skin tingles from widows peak to toes curled tight against peeling bark.

I'm snugged into a thick crook, hugging the trunk, head back and mouth open to better taste the ozone. To better smell the creosote, wet for thunder.

Want is deep in me like a jagged splinter, invisible pressure on a bundle of nerves, impossible to grasp with my fingers.

All I've known of sex is pain. Passive and stolen away. This rough tumbling of air and electricity, this press of sap and breath and gravity, is another channel entirely. I want to open up like roots to water. Want to climb the sky.

Pondering the nerve map of my muse

The process of writing is the same as peeling an apple, where the apple is your soul. Where the jagged strips flashing two distinct stories dangle from your own sharp teeth, worrying at truth like a bone. Always hungry for the marrow.

Ego fragments all through the core. Sometimes seeds, sometimes spaces where seeds couldn't grow. Sometimes rotted out to dry husk, waiting to be filled in. Prayed over. Let go.

Still chasing that truth. Still grinding teeth on gristle, hunting the echo of flavor. Of wind sound, of sky color, the meaning of his hand, her tears. The days I can't remember.

That scowling boy, was he huddled around his own pain? Children flinging words like knives, was it malice or fear? I make them uneasy, a young lion among gazelles. Smiling with these teeth too sharp for comfort, though I'd sooner chew my own mouth than attack.

Better that I had. Better I had gone down swinging then let myself be walled into a tiny space. Dim with all the corners where violation waits. Patient like the vultures. Better I had swallowed my own tongue then let them feel the weight of it.

This world flays me open, indifference like steel burrs across and across my tender heart. Like hate is easier. Like rage is easier. Like being jaded is a high art. Like 95% of us aren't even real.

What is the compensation of cruelty? What is the high of slicing someone down low? Why do the circles form around thumping cursing bodies, and why do mouths turn upward?

I would rather read you poetry. Feed you fresh baked bread, and apples drunk on honey. Light the flowers and send them upward, a prayer to laughter. Anoint sore flesh and bless it with gentle hands. Humming between these sharp teeth.

I have longed to tell the truth since I could speak. I have ached to know the why, to understand the who, to enfold the how. Pressing this peasant nose to the glass, straining every scrap of peripheral vision, trying to see the pattern. Trying to understand the reason for the blood.

There is not reason enough for the blood. There is not reason enough for the walls of broken houses, carving land into kingdoms, carving kings into bitter feasts.

And why kings. The false comfort of gender roles. The willful ignorance of diversity. And why the ruination of forests, of oceans, of skies. And why, ever why, again why.

I do not have a child's curiosity. That was lost with child's innocence. Child's wisdom. I do not have a child's grace. I barely had a child's face, except to hide behind. I seek out the truths worn into the roof of my mouth, unfold them, decipher what I can. I strip the apple.

My gender, in three parts

velvet survivor
gnarled anchor root
sinking thirsty deep
tender fertile filaments
dredging the wind
rose pink red petals
spicing the sweetness
thorns for self-care
schooling the greedy
medicine of aging
made beauty, wisdom
climbing the sky

piles of potatoes
sheen of butter like joy
and generosity
gentle precise knife
hand slicing fair
tongue smart and
gut wise, black truffle
green confetti of sage
rosemary, savory
a benediction
of breakfast, a
miracle of dinner

black leather boot stride
fishnets sing, torn, snug
against meaty thighs
leopard print cleavage
temple doors swung wide
sharp toothed smiling
brow arched steady
eye contact you will
flinch first and not
be sorry, even when
sorrowful or sore
truths spoken here

Magic formulas scrawled under cover of night

Roughclad iron bridge soaring above us. You towering above me. Such an angle on passion. My hands are hard around your thighs, yours in my hair. This is a breathless kiss. This is a gift. This is the first five minutes.

We arrived, into the shadows, walking from the north and the south.

No hesitation. Conversation had, lines drawn, all is play now. All is known, except, how long the tide will run. Until the waves rise up over this spot we have claimed. Your mouth on mine demanding kneeling, promising recompense.

Your shoulders captured me, before. Wide under a work shirt you actually work in. Ink marked and curling into arms quite long enough to wrap around these hips. To wrap around to wherever you need most to be. I'm clinging to those shoulders, now. Concrete pilings ruining the back of my dress. But I picked it for just such treatment. Will cut it into patchwork squares, later. Covering my bed with dreams of shameless pleasure.

There are no monsters underneath it except the moments that he stole. And also him. And also them.

You, me, this, is a spell. A banishment. A cleansing. With iron turning back into ore, with stars pushing past city lights, with our breath mingled.

Numbers have teeth

This feeling of shame that turns belly into burden. This way of standing (suck it in) of holding my face (tilt that chin) that sneaks up on me. In the midst of strangers, or under the gaze of too many men at once. A high school specter. A gym class mallet. Pounding in my veins like a migraine of the skin.

The literal weight of the meat and bone like a math problem. Where numbers have teeth but aren't supposed to use them. Except for smiling. When told to. You know.

(Such a pretty face.)
(She should feel lucky.)
(Looking the way she does.)

As if being deemed fuckable is a compliment. As if my fat cunt is currency with a low exchange rate. They make offers that slouch off the tongue. They expect fear, or gratitude.

(This knife in my bag.)
(These five work worn knuckles.)
(This sharp edged tongue.)

I give them as little as possible. Confine my rage to my eyes. Give them a chance to back away, so that I can come back. Claim this thick glory of mine. Let out my breath. Cradle my belly. Smile into my chins. (But not for them.) (Never for them.) The shame is not mine, it stains their hands.

Elemental

I exist where salvaged iron meets vintage porcelain
dropped, picked up, repaired, shared, dropped again
where rust kisses fractures salved with dime store glue
wet with the spit of a hundred days of dry mouth wishes
for answers, a place less brittle to rest my dreams
blood red fractals pierced with pain drawn in lines
that don't know how to be straight or clean or simple
bending slowly on cold mornings or maybe not at all
perfecting a place for words both shaky and defiant
sharp edged and refusing to submit to lockjaw
pits and grooves and a finish rubbed to wisdom
a learning of the deep ground, of the salt air
of the forging and the breaking, of the pause
on the cusp of each, and the hedonism embraced
despite the danger of falling, or being forgotten

I exist where mourning dove meets high flying moon
rounded, airborne, captured, whittled down to bone
where pink white curves kiss a blue expanse laid wide
surviving and risen from the knives into bloodred eclipse
singing my song of loss and want to the crying sky
courting tender clouds and sharp mountains alike
knowing their embraces differ only in the marks left
mouthing my marrow as if that were how love felt
eroding into a basin to hold all the sour and sweet
my tongue can't tell the difference when it moves
seeking and shouting and naming a faith found hard
a learning of the night wind, of the lightning
of the soaring and the plunging, of the pause
on the cusp of each, and the hedonism embraced
despite the danger of falling, or being forgotten

Some lessons take longer

I knew you for 10 years or maybe
never at all. No, that's anger.
Sorrow. I knew you when
you came to me in joy.

I knew the light in your eyes,
the hunger of your touch.

You sought me out like treasure.
Traveled for a year and a day
to the place you could show
yourself to me.

You offered love, offered
beauty and freedom and I
needed them and you
needed me.

Better partnered, you said.
I hate to cook, you said.
One bedroom is plenty, you said.

As if that was the whole story.
As if you weren't also a treasure.
As if you didn't give me all you had to give.

It just happened that your desire stopped growing,
and we ate all of mine. That you realized you
weren't feeling hungry anymore.

Said I should eat out.
But only on Tuesdays.
And don't like it too much.

Fasting meant I love you, meant
you were valued. Proved everyone who left
you hungry was wrong. Meant I understood.

Fasting meant nothing once I
couldn't anymore. One no to erase
a decade of yes. To erase me.

10 years later and I am still left
wondering if I ever could
have fasted, enough.

What portion of us
would have survived.
How bitter the taste.

Warning signs

my eyes are dry
my cunt is wet
my heart is ache
my fists are clench
my mouth is dry
my eyes are wet
my gut is roil
my grief is new
my eyes are dry
my bones are ache
my heart is full
my hands are not
my bones are old
my gut is clench
my cunt is dry
my eyes are wet
my voice is ache
my mouth is wet
my heart is roil
my grief is old

You're never really
listening to me

I forget that, over and over
and over and over and over

gone from your touch
my body, returns from
banishment

I'll never forget again
finally knowing

my heart my cunt my voice
my gut my bones my hands

Naked rebellion

Act one:

The first lesson I learned was the purity of hedonism, the feel of water on bare skin and a mouthful of comforting food and the slow tender rituals of hairbrushes and lullabies. The harbor of lap and the sanctity of eye contact, the dance of heat and cold and the shifting nature of breath and heartbeat. To notice, and noticing, give thanks, and thanking, to pass on and preserve. To pay forward, pay attention, pay homage to self without ego and others without possession. Giving openly for sake of giving.

Act two:

The hot springs are clothing optional, but some of us are still intended to be clothed in shame. To fold in on our folds, to cross our arms into curtains and pull those curtains into confessionals and keep our confessions to ourselves because they've already been written for us. I stand, stretch, slowly. Turn my back on their faces and leave them to gaze upon the tattoo emblazoned above the ass they would make me regret if they could. Tramp. My word, for my reasons. Stolen back and startling them into silence.

Act three:

The world is literally burning and the future looks bleak but I take nude photos of my lover in the garden. For now, we still have plants and trees, creatures and birds and bees. At some soon point the beauty of our bodies may simply be that they are still alive but for now, we navigate a world that deems them deviant, that shuns and mocks them. We, basking in sunshine that is yet bearable, glorying in air that is yet breathable, wearing grins and gratitude, bless them. Keep learning more about love and survival.

On staying in, again

I miss dancing. Not like water, or the vital breath of trees, but like the color blue only a desert can reflect. I miss the sharp edge of my smile carving out space for my hip, swinging into the shape of joy. I miss the slick smell of my own sweat, heart driven and salty.

> wanting so hard
> barely attainable
> powerless to change
> the nature of bones
> I tell myself
> that I hate bars

What I hate is that jarring edge of strange faces pushing into personal spaces. Violations of careless curiosity. My back against a wall, not dancing. Resting one leg at a time, the passing of so many indifferent eyes like dust in my throat. My stars too dim to see.

> this is a song
> of twitch and sigh
> sung on any key
> that will hold itself up
> this is a story
> I tell myself

Remembering the twirl of my skirt in a waltz. The shine of 50 silver studs on boots that slide just right. The spiritual rush of funk. The grit of rock. The soul driven arch of my back stealing words from my lovers mouth while their hands hold my waist like they might drown.

Unfruit

My
body
rejects
standards
constantly
even those of
biology, my uterus
dropping this useless
wad of meat, heavy and
misshapen nothing at all
like a grapefruit or a child
product of a thwarted maker
this dangling twisted knot
muscle and fibers serving no
purpose, crowding my organs
seizing up every tender place
walking and sex and sitting
and working and not crying
endurance tests or impossible
and my isolation grows bigger
centimeters at a time along with
fear and worry, sorrow, exhaustion
and loss, to think I was mourning
my ability to dance and now I
just want to go 1 hour without
having to pee, stand up without
making involuntary sounds
hurt and betrayal, ripping
and root bound inside
my own tender skin

Spelling of my name

I've been told I sometimes look
like I would eat you up
like I would suck your bones
clean
and hollow
leave you flying
high and rune marked

it's true
I love the meat of you
miles of magic
woven just under the skin
I love my teeth
swirling across your landscape
lightning and flash floods

four pearled inches
held in check
around soft slow licks
that take all three breaths
you'll forget to breathe
to get from collarbone
to jugular

like just now
when you gulped
oxygen, trying hard for subtle
as if you weren't trying
to get my sharp attention
as if you hadn't flapped
your signal flag like a flare

the tang of pheromones
sweat gathered
into the small of your back
thin skin stretched taut
fluttering with your pulse
morse of ache to read with my tongue
tip butterfly soft and merciless

if it is 10 minutes
I will make it feel like an hour
if it is an hour
I will make it feel like a freight train
if it is a freight train
your cells will know I love you
and the spelling of my name

Lineage

Comfort and curse words on the wire, stretching from my isolation to hers. Nobody has ever understood us the way we do, and don't we wish they could. Veil torn from her eyes at 8 years old and struggling ever since to understand how so many can refuse to see. How hate can root in deep and grow, how violence becomes the currency and the debt. All the ways humans can lay waste to their humanity, and each other. To ourselves. We see it.

We breathe ragged deep together, echoing across the electronic umbilical, and the distance aches to the bone. We share tips on how to not give up on humans. To not give up. We share our treasure hoard of bird friends and flowers, mantras for grace and resilience. We trace the shapes of lonely and left behind, of the precious few that still show up. Patch them into sandbags. Pile them around doors we leave open, or close gently, or barricade.

She offers to share the playlist of happy memory songs. Ones she plays when the immense sorrowful weight of it all buries her under a pile of blankets and despair. Explains it's also for her going away party. How she wants us to sing and dance and remember and grieve and comfort each other. I listen as best I can with hands gripping the arms of my chair like a cliff face. The thought of losing her going through the center of me with serrated edges.

She can't possibly know the fear of that. She can't possibly not know. Breathe in. Listen. Stay present. She deserves a joyful leave taking when the time comes. She deserves to create the container to hold her safely home. She is sharing this vulnerable truth with me because she knows I can bear it. We both can bear so much. The wire bends under the enormity of trust and hope. Bends but does not break. Blessing, not burden.

She knows. My whole life, every sorrow or soaring. Every scar.
She has witnessed every unfolding to a deeper knowing of self.
Celebrated it. Leaned into the overlap. Learned all that lays outside
it. Stretched her understanding to encompass me. Laid her own
longing and fear and courage and survival strategies on the table.
Offered me a chair. We can fall apart together. We know where the
pieces go.

Our chemistries differ. Words tumble and layer and never quite
capture the fullness of what she wants to share. They have long
been my steady thing, polished and explored down to the pores. I
lay them out in precisely syncopated patterns. She gathers them in
bunches, piled high and dropping blossoms and seed heads. Behind
her eyelids are worlds rich in color and texture. Behind mine are
darkness and the imagining of things.

Bodies like twin peaks in a mountain range. We know the
mudslides of muscle ache and the tremors of pain below. We know
exhaustion like a ravine shadowed fully from the sun. Fault lines
and fertile riverbeds. Springs wild passion and winters dim despair.
Spangled caverns of strength and minerals that should never have
been mined. Bedrock solid and autumn leaf surrender. Sometimes
soft moss. Sometimes sharp thorn. We breathe together.

In the red

There is a math to the body
and not just those microscopic geometries
that make up our very cells
that mimic the stars
that are the starstuff
and not just those snowflake bits
our irregular asymmetries
that catch the eye
but don't add up to just one sum
and not just those tide pattern whorls
marking every digit in every one
or even those fortune telling tributaries
spilling into the creases across lifeblood

there is the math of how much it can take
how much it can give, and how long
it's a complex formula, so many variables
drawn from a lottery of class, race, geography
it is most definitely a math of story problems

if you have one child born into poverty
funneled into manual labor, say, housecleaning
how many times can they do that
with their one pair of shoulders?
And it's not just the math of what they do for you
there are lovers to rock and art to make and
dancing to do and babies to lift and don't forget
their own house to clean with shoulders so sore
and it's not just the math of how long they can work
but also do they get to eat, and are drugs cheaper than hope
four pairs of shoes plus two pairs of glasses plus five winter coats
because that neighbor kid is minus one parent to prison
and it isn't charity if you've looked each other in the eye

the math of our system is imbalanced
does not add up, demands that this 1
is worth 20 billion, and that 1 is really a zero
does not care about balance, only sums
where greater than eats everything

The world eats Femmes and I am left hungry

My heart is a ragged thing. Scars raised raw, fading echoes. There is
no song that can convey the sound of her voice. The strength of
her choice. She said it's time. She said I love you. She ate the deadly
pudding. My ears are empty, the sound is lost.

I swallow, I swallow, I stumble through the day. I make myself
eat. I chase sleep into the small hours. I wash my salt burned face.
Rearrange it into grace. Swallow my sobs. Change the radio station.
Change the subject. The sound is lost. My heart is a ragged thing.

Her voice is part of a chorus. Falling too soon through the cracks
of a broken system. Sucked dry and left empty. Poisoned and
silenced. A diagnosis of lies. Dismissed when she cries. My heart is
a ragged thing, the sound is lost, she is gone. I swallow, I swallow.

I stumble through the day. Looking skyward, seeking hope. I hold
the ones still earthbound. I hold myself. I trace the scars. I set them
among the stars. I stitch my heart together, tune it to echoes. I sing
a ragged song. Her voice is part of a chorus.

Begging for the teeth of grief

Sometimes it bites down hard
shakes you like a rag doll
and: you let it, arms and legs loose
rib cage rattling
because you can't stand to hold it in
because you can't stand
because you can't
stand it
and: the shaking is like rocking
for just a moment
like a lap and a chair and a song
but less tender
more truth
more train tracks
less teddy bear
until: your heart
crouches on your tongue
and the tears
break your nose
or is that your breath
or is that the sound of a closed door
jumping hinges rusted shut
so: it all rushes in
sorrow and guilt and anger and regret
longing and a bit of wild sharp wit
escaping
flailing arms
can't force it down
groundless legs
can't run away
so: nape high, chin set
begging for the teeth of grief
you wait
hoping for a take down
a knockout stumble
into slumber
respite from the knowing
all the chances spent, slipped away
through the ragged shape of gone

Confession

your tipped fedora smile
and bourbon spiked voice
drive my '46 mercury body
around every curve of this road
foot relaxed over the pedals
hands easy on the wheel
no way to know if you'll
put on the brakes
or speed us up and over the hill
it's a delicious not-knowing
that makes my smile so wide
it reflects this blue moon
while my hair blows
in the soft wind
of your satisfied chuckle
it is a creation myth
it is a fairy tale
it is improv theater
comedy
open mic
confession

it is the longing of atoms
and a primate's dream
it is heady gender
tender feelings
life worn flesh
trusting
and flying
or falling
as the lesson requires
it is old family dynamics
and new disappointments
it is art, heart and soul
it is bone, blood and philosophy
it is oxygen
it is prayer

you clasp my fingers
put them into your mouth
taste the musk and hope
I left there for you
you show me your scar
that leads to desire
you teach me the rhythm
that finds your glory
you sing me your song
I don't know the words
but my hum satisfies
and I learn with repetition

we roll to a gentle stop
stretch our legs
catch our breath
then come together
iron to magnet
a joyous collision

I let you see my shadow
the one that shows in the dark
the one that lights the path
if you find it
put your hand, over my heart
twist, just so
and release
if you listened
it will open
pour out my
divine beast
my
fearsome
gentle
knowledge
all the characters
that can hold my

spirit
and hunger
the tapestry
of self
that I would share
let you
finger my knots

tangle yourself
in my unraveled edges

braid a rope to bind me
down
to
set me free
to
hold back my hair
while you kiss your way
along the nape of my neck
over my shoulder
to that spot where your teeth
bring submission
a pleasure akin
to gazing at the sun
for just a second
dazzled and
boundless
no ground
no sky
simply skin
and what is against it
your weight
pressing me into the dirt
your entrance
like lightning
striking
the same place twice

bonfire
brushfire
conflagration
of cool waves
washing me
sacred
I am, you are
we are
sanctified
outlaw

Yearning for Brigid

I have written almost as many poems about pain
as I have about love, have explored the jagged lines
it writes on my bones, the isolation and exhaustion
have questioned divinity, my sanity, and the systems
we call heathcare, though they are often careless
seeing my fat and ignoring my muscles, though the first
cradles my sore joints and the second pull them sideways
shudder quakes across my pelvic floor sending me into shock
and awe at how fiery a body made of mostly water can feel
Spending out hundreds of dollars to educate doctors
on courtesy and collusions of class and access, on listening
hoping for kindness, for a clearer view of the next body
that shows up seeking comfort and answers at their door
I strip myself more naked than any hospital gown could
begin to cover, speak truths they flinch from, frowning

I have written almost as many poems about pain
as I have about the decaying state of the world trying
to survive the grinding on of capitalism and corporate
definitions of value, the plunder and power of profit
Roughshod trampling marginalized bodies and medicine
sacrificed on the opioid altar, another offering to
the impotent omnipotence of insurance companies
god of numbers crunching deviation into bloody ink
to illustrate and annotate the bible of the bottom line
with a cover made of midwives and old wives and lost
lives in the pursuit of a perfection that is inhuman and
inhumane, that is so much less beautiful than genuine
imperfection and healing that is holistic, that is the very
meaning of poetry, the energy and atoms and compassion
the connection, the reasons we find for continuing to be

Too complex for father

1. I am over 50, and still grieving for two fathers who chose me, and then chose not me.
2. One didn't choose to father me, didn't try, left, came back, left again, and likely won't return.
3. One chose to father me, tried hard, stopped trying, left, and made it clear he won't return.
4. They are both still alive, and so am I, but there is only silence.
5. Both of them know I'm deviant but have no idea how much so.
6. One might not judge but never bothered to learn.
7. One finds what little they do know to already be too much.
8. My greatest gifts and beauty are my deviance.
9. They don't see either, for failing to look, or refusing to.
10. Thinking about them fills with me with rage and sorrow.
11. Movies about good fathers make me cry.
12. My partner's loving father makes me cry and smile.
13. My brothers being wonderful fathers makes me cry and proud.
14. I am tired of the envious echoing depth of abandonment.
15. I am tired of the taste of salt.
16. I am tired.
17. I have always felt like an outsider.
18. This list doesn't begin to capture the feel of it.
19. I keep typing, because it feels less powerless than more crying.
20. I've stopped typing at least 10 times already.
21. One spoke to me a half a dozen times ever, but not for decades.
22. Dropped me when I dropped his name.
23. One hasn't spoken to me for years, or really known me for decades.
24. Dropped me when I dropped truth bombs.
25. 53 years of life, with maybe 15 years of parenting combined.
26. Numbers are an illusion of control.
27. Memories are an illusion of comfort.
28. I grieve but I do not wait for them.
29. I do not wait for them to grieve me.
30. Unlike this list, I continue on.

Rock out, stuck in

The pain is so loud I want to scream, break things,
knock down walls and I can't even walk without lurching

I crank the Led Zeppelin up extra loud and rock in this chair
tap the foot on the leg that isn't aching today and remember

the feel of mosh pit, the feel of folding into meditation pose, of
running and wrestling and dancing and loving so hard

Crank the music up louder, press hard on my forehead
Drown out the fear, shake in this chair and remember

Not to bite my own lip until it bleeds even though blood
is a satisfaction I remember, like dance
is a joy I remember like walking for miles

is a freedom I remember, crank the music up louder
tap into the feeling of before pain, before the compromises

When movement was simple, when my body was newly reclaimed
strong and supple and ready to move or relax into stillness

too much stillness now, feels like stagnant, feels like thwarted, feels
like I don't get to choose, or like choosing is preservation not
exploration

I need hard edges, need to throw myself around and scream at the sky
Need the salt of hours of sex, of being on hands and knees gardening

I'm singing along like the howl of a wolf left lonely, like
the leaves of a willow weeping in a storm, like
nobody is listening because I can't leave the house

crank the music up louder, the tears pressing harder until
my face cracks wide open and sobbing along,
until the shatter is outside more than in

Sorrow and Sacred Places

I.

Ash is falling
not at all like snow
hazing a hot orange sun
angry, impossible
to watch, or look away
bodies of a million trees
mixing with deer and bee
fern and bear and mushroom
hungry flames devouring
acre upon acre of land
stolen so many times
we believe it belongs
to us, none of this
belongs to us
we weep and choke
on ghosts and call it smoke
our brand-new grief
laid down on the ash
of land we still desecrate
people we still terrorize
our brand-new grief
born from carelessness
like a firecracker off a cliff
or the destruction of entire
forests, stripped down to
furniture and fence posts
we rip holes in the sky
the ground, whole
continents of people
with sharp edged greed
and fail in our apologies

II.

Ash in the sky
and a dying molar
in my mouth
both taste bitter
like drying tears
and the truth
we're a jumble
of disparate cogs
churning out broken
bodies and phantom
bootstraps, shame
as currency and
grease, the wheels
turn every beautiful
thing into money
paper dry, burning holes
in pockets, and skies
turn cultures into
commerce, an exchange
rate that favors ghosts
but only when mute
hung like trophies
and the hunt never ends
we are fish in a barrel
paying for water
they tell us harpoons
are ladders, laugh
when we bleed

III.

Ash spreads like
panic, a state
struggling to breathe
to believe
that the blue sky
will come again
that anything sacred
green and wonderful
will be waiting
chests aching hungry
for oxygen and hope
fill with anger
wound tight, breath
heavy and hot
forced in past teeth
grit flecked with
wood, bone, ghosts
on the wind, sharp
when we swallow
tracking tears
across jawlines
and dim streets
full of people
with nowhere
to shelter

Meat truths

Pressing hard on the pulse at my neck, thumb thumping vibration. Walking the boundary of self-harm. Proving my existence, plumbing how far below the surface I might be. Feeling the blood they didn't take yet. Scouring it for markers of what is wrong with me, another tangled string in the snarl. Binding me into fearful mysteries and out of control. I press and I find it again.

As a child I tested my edges in liquid wax. Fingertips feeling no heat. The skin becoming thicker. Delicate spirals of identity encased. No longer exposed. I stitched across my palm. Tiny needle, shallow dipping below down and in and out again. Head line. Heart line. Life line. I wrapped a string round and round, my finger turning red, then white, then numb. Like my own places of pleasure. Like my voice.

I wanted to know the meat truths of me. To have power of sensation. Of taking and giving and when to stop. That I could make it stop. To know if it was math, or chaos, and how to survive either. To find the tools to build a moat. A gate. A lock. To feel all of one piece. Gather up the parts that were stolen. The places that were mined. The innocence I never knew was treasure until it became plunder.

Flesh as a map. This scar, that flinch, this wrinkle, that resilience. Razed and replanted. Volcanos and earthquakes and mudslides. Fossils and flowers. Anointed by lovers singing songs of grace and electricity. Distorted by their fears until only breaking the mirror would do. Decried by strangers preaching horrors of hedonism unleashed and infertile. Invaded and invalidated and impressed their hate upon it.

Making magic spells out of reclamation. Stopping myself, as many times as it takes, of thinking about that time. His enormous hands and my tiny body. The shattering and the slipping away. I gather the fragments. I light the candles. Banish the shadows. Salt the water, scatter the rose petals, step in as slowly as I need. Keep my eyes open and the front door locked. Keep a heavy stone in every room, close at hand.

Trauma nested deep, lunging out to crumble me into panic. My back to the wall. A knife by my bed. In my bag. Under my tongue. I keep the safety chain on when I open my heart. I keep trying not to dream. Almost always hunted, or lost, or vulnerable. Unable to find anyone safe. Unlit unknown streets and a phone that never works. Strangers wearing familiar faces, breaking trusts. Loneliness. Danger. Despair.

Can't run or fight like I used to, but I'd break my body to defend it. Made my own armor, wear it like a warning. Leather boots, steel cane, sharp teeth. I know all too well the tender places where nerves or blood are just below the skin. I know how to make you stop. How to make you sorry you started. How to make sure you remember and regret me. I will never go softly again.

Until I cry

you know my bone
deep need to let go
and the walls the world
builds around tears

tension building
twanging nerves
taut
from holding
firm
against intrusion
so many eyes boring
inside my clothes
on the street no
escape
just resistance
building up
gummy and
bitter choking
joy

until pounded
washed clean
with sweet salt
water
unleashed by
carefully rough
completely skilled
lock picking
fingers

opening me like
a window onto
spring rain every
drop a testament

sometimes it's like
a deep sea
dive
down into murky
cold layers childhood
sorrows
adult hazards broken
cutting edges
lurking beneath

your hands are
torches
in the darkness
nets to drag
and catch old
shards dredging
them up into
sunlight
while the dirt
settles softer now
cleaner each time

becoming just
earth in water
a growth medium
not quicksand

Lessons I'm learning from my garden

1. Roses don't survive because they are beautiful. Their roots are deep and stubborn, twisting underground, foot by unlit foot. Bypassing borders and paths altogether. Pushing up through domesticated landscapes into a spot of sunlight they choose. They bloom as resistance. They hook their thorns into thin air and climb the sky.

2. Spiders turn persistence into art. Sustain themselves on trespassers, and refuse to smile.

3. Weeds carry the wisdom of the elders they'd have us forget. Handfuls of color and mouthfuls of flavor. Medicine mowed under and returning stronger than before. Outlaws seeding intuition.

Haunted

My body is brimming with ghosts, by which I mean trauma and injury and pain and illness and loss and generational memory but

also this sliver of cadaver bone in my jaw, rooting into the space where my own teeth used to be.

Poverty and genetics and capitalism and trauma converging into the size of 4 molars that survived it all with me, until recently.

Stitches running through my gum, holding in the sliver and the ghosts and my tongue keeps creeping over, fascinated with and forbidden from the empty space.

The sutures that shouldn't be there and the teeth that should.

There are ghosts in this house, but they aren't mine. Except the one in the bathroom which has travelled with me since I was five.

When innocence died on white tiles at the feet of the man who took from me what I never offered. What I have never been able to resurrect.

Water is my comfort and my shelter, forever fraught. Each bath wrested from shadows and memory that I fought to get back and fight to keep silent.

Each shower with my eyes wide open and a heartbeat I focus on, keeping it steady and anchored in the present.

Ghosts inhabit my dreams, riding nightmares roughshod through my tender brain.

My breathing stops hundreds of times in a night, which is both a medical thing and also a reflection of how my dreams are spent.

Even with the new emptiness, my mouth is small and my curious tongue falls back and down and shocks up and away and falls again. Gravity and ghosts,

siphoning oxygen and rest so that I rise with weary salted eyes. I have become a diver at night, air flowing steady and strapped to my face, banishing gravity but not ghosts.

My bones harbor ghosts. They wind down from my skull, whispering of assaults and all the movements lost to me.

Gnawing on my shoulders, they wake me at 3am, dragging my arms into trenches of ache and thwarted. Crawling into my hips, they taunt dance and sex and stairs and long walks.

They resist the pleasure I chase there, driving sharp points into soft edges.

They spin nests in my knees, tangled wires and broken glass. They carve ridges in my forearms. Stitching my wrists and hands into shapes that hold little of the grace of flight.

The winding hallways of my brain hide ghosts in pockets of shadow, springing forth in unguarded moments and scattering fear and doubt like landmines.

Paths that were safe yesterday blow holes in my certainty today, sorrow and anxiety shrapnel through my thoughts until the only safety is silence.

Isolation is not exorcism.

The ghosts dissipate and lay in wait. They mutter to themselves in corners and mock their gaze across my efforts.

They dig muddy holes and wallow in them, tracking dirty across joy. I break the chains and shred the sheets and try again.

Communion

I want to feel your tongue between the folds
of my back, delving for mysteries beyond language
hands gripping tight to hips dancing against your chest
while teeth that long for your bicep make do with a pillow
oxygen a joyful sacrifice until you softly roll me over

eyes caressing the waterfall of my belly rising
up to your hungry hands, burrowing
for the wet heat heart of me, tender and fierce
as the formless sounds that sing from my mouth
swollen and curved and shameless

one two three quick slaps to starry constellations
on thighs that have rubbed a thousand miles
through a world that sees me less as my flesh
grows more, that would rob that beauty you see
and leave me hollowed out and stuffed with shame

but your hungry hands write stories of glory
on the scrolls of fat, passed down through
generations of peasants and priestesses
magic spells woven of raw silk and sweet butter
melting on the altar of your tongue

4 planets in retrograde and a manbaby in the white house

living in moments where clarity becomes chaos, where chaos becomes potential, where potential is another string of words to fill the space between what was and what will now never be. where heartbreak and fresh start are uneasy synonyms.

> where I am not at all where I thought I would be,
> no more certain of the future but no more lost
> than ever I am in my own skin, looking forward.

living in moments where hope feels dangerous, but oh so necessary. where the end is possibly upon us but we have no more control than ever. where we have a louder voice than ever. where we wonder what we even means anymore, and fight. pray. for it to mean something.

> where I am still alive, decades longer than I ever expected
> and life feels fragile and ferocious and I am limping
> and roaring and hungry for more.

living like the privilege it is. like the battleground it is. like the blessing and the curse and the wonder and the misery and the mystery that it is. like I choose it, keep choosing it, have struggled with choosing it, may someday not choose it, but right now, for as long as I can, I do.

Balance

There's a price on these parts
no matter how empty my pockets
the sums of bills upon bills, written
on the outer edge of my eyelid
so it twitch twitch twitches
towards the end of the month
and I squint through the quivers
at this glowing screen, headaches
a couple times a week at least, still
better than a hand gone numb
around my pen, and a poem stillborn
on the paper, nothing but flat blue lines
because the grinding of joints is loud
and frozen all at once, like polar ice
and the keyboard is just a dull ache, cheap
in comparison, though the right forearm
is all used up, left hand on the mouse
coerced into ambidextrous, tiny clicks
that cost hours on the massage table, deep
pressing fingers and elbows to dig out the
ridges of fascia, fused by repeatedly pushing
too far, to find art, and rent, and this voice
that is weighed against bone and vision
and wins every time, this voice
that is all the truest parts of me,
down to the sore depths
until my blood stands still

Upon being high risk in a disputed pandemic

Eating the crumbs dropped from tables with no room for us. Trod and spat upon as they are. Being told to stop complaining. That we're lucky to get anything at all, inconvenient as we are. Disposable people should always be grateful.

Don't live in fear. Don't name where it comes from. Don't describe the way it breathes down the back of your neck, all droplets and deception. Don't air your nightmares out loud, naked faces all around. No masks and no escape.

My gut thrashes. Instinct and observation and isolation. Mourning and raging on a shrinking shore. All the people who have set sail for normal and left us to drown. Tossing life jackets and logic overboard to safeguard the vibe.

Outlaw linguistics

Feminine thinks I belong to them, but I'm not doing it right. Femme seeks to set me free, and knows however I do it is my right way. Feminine is a cog in the system, cut to fit, the slot for the tab. Femme is the wrench in the gears, the dismantling of locks into adornment and armor.

Feminine is to Femme as a neon light is to the aurora borealis. Which is to say, a created sense of garish meant as job security, rather than the natural wonder of the world showing off entirely for their own pleasure. Which is to oversimplify everything, in the pursuit of explaining one thing.

Feminine is has been will be was always divine. The familiar and the mysterious. The object of desire, but no, we keep telling you, not object. Subject. Not meant to be a reflection of the will and the rules and the force of masculine. Femme rejects biological imperative and capitalistic agendas.

Feminine is to phrase as Femme is to verb. The improper noun and an independent clause. Femme diagrams the sentence, turns it into a dress pattern, turns that into a paper airplane, flies it around the world, turns it back into a sentence, and ends in a defiant ellipsis.

Femme is very inclusive, but not of everybody. Femme is a gender. Femme is not found in breasts or cunts or high heels or pantyhose or conventional gender markers or endless youth or homogeneous beauty. Femme is not found at all, it is created. Femme is an art form.

Femme is the vessel of clay, shaped between palms seeking to love, under pressure, burnished into being through testing flames and chemical reactions, bearing up through feasts and fear and famines and fury. Chipped and seamed and run through with precious metals and shoplifted glue.

Femme is not for the taking. Not the bodies, not the word. Femme is to feminine like essay question is to multiple choice. Like all you can eat is to calorie counting. Like the big box of crayons is to a piece of chalk. You can create beauty with that chalk, but in limited ways.

Femme is tools for dismantling, down to the bones, and fibers for building back up again. Each piece considered, chosen, or discarded. Building a new framework to hang a life upon. To weave through with community and connection, with art and activism, with the treasure that is self.

Feminine can be has been will become many of these things. Can challenge and change and choose. Can be the verb and the subject and the art form. Feminine can make of itself something like Femme, but if it is not queer, or if it is not trans, it is not Femme. It is some other beautiful thing.

Of moonlight and roses and mammals

brow furrowed
you delve inside me
for stories of coral
and kelp
the slippery grasp
of forever

of your own
desire, deep
set and hard
thrusting tectonic
quaking, but
I'm not talking
about science

I am sweat wet
mammal
climbing your arm

I am howling
your face is the moon
your face   is the moon

your smile a burst of stars
through the thin skin
of my eyelids
hot washed and
half mast
seeking you

a watery moon
an ocean
I open to

my cunt grown
to the size of
your heart

I am a drum ba
drum brum brum come
come coming

again words like:
vibration
yowl
salt

wet meat   wide open

you stroll you skip you jog you run
you pause   you pause
you dash in lead boots then slow

my cunt is a cave
a grove around that cave
the sky above that grove

my cunt is home

your hands are the wind
late night lock picking
breezes

rustling my shades
to rolling, over
slapping sounds
and flashes of
streetlight
wide open

and again, metaphor
when what I mean is
fucking

what I mean is
on your arm
I am a bouquet
of thorny rose
I am storm cloud
whistle and whirl
I am sobbing
your name

Special thanks

In this time of great uncertainty and possibility, I want to humbly thank my non-human community members. I am profoundly grateful for the gift of engaging with life that is bigger, older, and infinitely more balanced, despite our species' worst behavior.

I rest quiet in the presence of buds returning and dropping leaves. Slowly mouth the sweetness of berry and sun beam. Bathe in the sacred of rain water dripping through pine. I pledge to follow the example of the squirrel in playful and persistence. The crows in resistance and solidarity. The bees in collaboration and transformation. To be ungovernable as dandelion and resilient as rose.

Acknowledgments

I have so much appreciation for all the journals and anthologies and editors that have made a space for my work, including the following from this collection:

- "Meat Truths" – *Wishbone Words*
- "Lineage" – *Hndl Magazine*
- "In the red" — *F(r)iction*
- "Confession" - *Adrienne Journal*
- "Until I cry," "On staying in, again," "My gender, in three parts" and "Magic formulas scrawled under cover of night" – *Flannel Mag*
- "Numbers have teeth" — Unchaste *Readers Series: Volume 1*
- "Balance" — *The Other Side of Violet*
- "Lessons I learned from my garden" —*Unchaste Readers Series: Volume 3*
- "Rock out, stuck in" — *Rogue Agent*
- "Outlaw linguistics" and "Of Moonlight and roses and mammals" — *Crab Fat*

About the Author

photo by Yaara Perczek @tenderheartphoto

Sossity Chiricuzio (she/they) is a fat femme outlaw poet, a working class crip storyteller. What her friend's parents often referred to as a bad influence and possibly still do. She is the author of the memoir *Honey & Vinegar: Recipe for an Outlaw* (Beaten Track Publishing, 2019), and the poetry collection *Stir the Juice* (self-published, 2013). A Lambda Fellow and a sensitivity reader at Writing Diversely, Sossity writes as activism, connection, and survival. Her work can be found in a variety of publications including *Stirring, Salty, The Rumpus, Lunch Ticket, Rogue Agent, Library Journal,* and *Rooted in Rights,* as well as anthologies like *The Remedy: Queer and Trans Voices on Health and Health Care, Glitter and Grit: Queer Performance from the Heels on Wheels Femme Galaxy,* and *Not My President.*

Sossity was sainted by the Sisters of Perpetual Indulgence for their work hosting and producing Dirty Queer, a long running open mic focused on sex, gender, and sexuality. That tiny stage brought about big community connections, fundraising, writing workshops, and more than a few romances. To this day, friendly strangers will approach saying "Dirty Queer!?"

She weaves outside the lines as Warped Femme, which is an art therapy and community service practice with all proceeds going directly to relief and resources for marginalized people. Sossity can talk about snakes, native plants, and sci-fi for hours, but luckily her partner Max can too (maybe not so much the plants), and the two of them are often found collaborating on fiber art, mutual aid, and songwriting for their performance duo Sparkle & truth.

Find out more at sossitywrites.com.

Other Poetry by Echobird Press

The Gatekeeper Wears Acrylics by Court Winterborne
the bones of this land by Kat Heatherington
A Map Without Your Shadow by Kat Heatherington
No Longer Water by Katrina Kaye

ECHOBIRD
PRESS

Fiction by Echobird Press

Friends With Wings by Maxwell Pearl
The Artifact by Maxwell Pearl (forthcoming May 2025)
The Alters series by Terra Katherine McKeown